CALL TO RESCUE, CALL TO HEAL
Emergency Medical Professionals at Ground Zero

FIRST TO ARRIVE
Firefighters at Ground Zero

GUARDIANS OF SAFETY
Law Enforcement at Ground Zero

HELPING HANDS
A City and a Nation Lend Their Support at Ground Zero

KEEPING THE PEACE
The U.S. Military Responds to Terror

WE THE PEOPLE
The U.S. Government's United Response Against Terror

United We Stand
AMERICA RESPONDS TO THE EVENTS OF
September 11, 2001

WE THE PEOPLE

The U.S. Government's United Response Against Terror

Angela Valdez

CHELSEA HOUSE
PUBLISHERS
A Haights Cross Communications Company

PHILADELPHIA

FRONTIS: President George W. Bush descending the steps of Air Force One. In the hours immediately following the September 11 attacks, the nation turned to the president for inspiration and leadership and setting the stage for one of the most important tests of the new administration.

CHELSEA HOUSE PUBLISHERS

EDITOR IN CHIEF Sally Cheney
DIRECTOR OF PRODUCTION Kim Shinners
CREATIVE MANAGER Takeshi Takahashi
MANUFACTURING MANAGER Diann Grasse

STAFF FOR WE THE PEOPLE

ASSOCIATE EDITOR Benjamin Xavier Kim
PICTURE RESEARCHER Sarah Bloom
PRODUCTION ASSISTANT Jaimie Winkler
COVER AND SERIES DESIGNER Keith Trego
LAYOUT 21st Century Publishing and Communications, Inc.

A Haights Cross Communications ✦ Company

http://www.chelseahouse.com

First Printing

1 3 5 7 9 8 6 4 2

Library of Congress Cataloging-in-Publication Data applied for.

Valdez, Angela.
   We the people : the U.S. government's united response against terror /
Angela Valdez.
      p. cm.—(United we stand)
Includes index.
Summary: Chronicles the response of the United States government to
the terrorist attacks of September 11, 2001.
   ISBN 0-7910-6962-1 (hardcover)—ISBN 0-7910-7183-9 (pbk.)
   1. Terrorism—Government policy—United States—Juvenile literature.
2. September 11 Terrorist Attacks, 2001—Juvenile literature. 3. War
on Terrorism, 2001– —Juvenile literature. [1. Terrorism—Government
policy. 2. September 11 Terrorist Attacks, 2001. 3. War on Terrorism,
2001–] I. Title. II. Series.
HV6432 .V35 2002
973.931—dc21
                                                    2002008252

TABLE OF CONTENTS

FOREWORD by Benjamin Xavier Kim   **6**

THE FIRST DAY   **9**

A HISTORY OF CRISIS SITUATIONS   **17**

THE KEY PLAYERS   **25**

SUPPORT FOR THE WAR ON TERROR   **33**

DOMESTIC SECURITY   **41**

ONGOING EFFORTS   **49**

WEBSITES   **56**

ORGANIZATIONS AND AGENCIES   **57**

FURTHER READING   **58**

BIBLIOGRAPHY   **59**

INDEX   **61**

Foreword

The events of September 11, 2001 will be remembered as one of the most devastating attacks on American soil ever. The terrorist attacks caused not only physical destruction but also shattered America's sense of safety and security, and highlighted the fact that there were many groups in the world that did not embrace the United States and its far-reaching influence. While things have, for the most part, returned to normal, there is still no escaping the demarcation of life before and after September 11—the newest day that will forever live in infamy.

Yet, even in the aftermath of the terror and destruction, one can see some positive effects that have arisen from the attacks. Americans' interest in foreign countries—especially those where Islam is the predominant religion—and U.S. foreign policy has been at an all-time high. The previously mundane occupations of firefighter, police officer and emergency medical worker have taken on a newfound level of respect due to the heroism and selflessness displayed on September 11. The issue of airport security has finally been taken seriously with

the implementation of National Guardsmen in airports and undercover air marshals aboard flights.

The books in this series describe how various groups and agencies dealt with the unfolding events of September 11. They also tell the history of these agencies and how they have dealt with other crises in the past, as well as how they are operating in the wake of September 11.

While the rest of us were reeling in shock and horror at what was unfolding before our eyes, there were others whose jobs required that they confront the situation head-on. These are their stories.

Benjamin Xavier Kim
Series Editor

The terrorist attacks on the World Trade Center and the Pentagon on September 11, 2001 shattered America's sense of security, and had many wondering what other buildings might be targets for similar attacks.

The First Day

On September 11, 2001, the United States awoke to a terrifying aerial attack on the centers of its military and financial power. Nineteen terrorists hijacked four commercial airliners and crashed the planes into the World Trade Center in New York City, the Pentagon in the nation's capital and a field in rural Pennsylvania. Thousands of civilians and military personnel were killed in the span of a few hours.

The first impact came at 8:46 A.M. when American Airlines Flight 11, a Boeing 767 en route from Boston to Los Angeles, struck the north tower of the World Trade Center, a sparkling glass complex in lower Manhattan that held office space for 50,000 workers. Eighteen minutes later, United Airlines Flight 175, also flying from Boston to Los Angeles, slammed into the south tower. The twin towers, once the tallest skyscrapers in the United States, swayed and burned, as desperate people jumped from top floors. At 9:50 A.M., as millions watched on national television, the south tower crumbled to the ground in a smoldering implosion of ash and twisted steel. The north tower collapsed at 10:28.

Almost an hour earlier, at 9:40 A.M., American Airlines flight 77, headed to Los Angeles from Washington's Dulles International Airport, flew off course and crashed into the western side of the Pentagon, the headquarters of the U.S. military. Part of the fortress collapsed.

It is believed that in a heroic effort, the passengers of the fourth airliner, United Airlines Flight 93, a Boeing 757 flying from Newark to San Francisco, perished when they forced their hijackers to crash the plane in rural Pennsylvania.

Two hundred and sixty six passengers and crewmembers died aboard the four planes. While estimates continue to be revised, more than 3,000 people are believed to have died on the ground. The massive number of casualties represents the most deadly individual assault on U.S. soil. Nothing could have prepared the American public or its leaders for the emotional impact of such devastation. Still, officials had plans in place to deal with disaster. And in the days and months that followed, that system was put to the test.

The U.S. response to the attacks began even before the first plane slammed into the south tower. Unfortunately, officials learned of the threats too late to make a difference.

At 8:40 A.M., the North American Aerospace Defense Command (NORAD), a bi-national organization charged with defending the airspace over the United States and Canada, was informed by the Federal Aviation Administration of the hijacking of United Airlines Flight 11. Six minutes later, NORAD ordered two F-15 Eagle fighter jets from Otis Air Force Base in Cape Cod to head for New York City.

By the time the jets were airborne, Flight 11 had slammed into the north tower. When Flight 175 hit the south tower, the Eagles were still 70 miles away.

At 9:24 NORAD learned that another flight might be headed toward Washington D.C. and ordered two F-16 Fighting Falcons into the air. But Flight 77 slammed into the Pentagon just 15 minutes later.

At about 8:30 A.M. on September 11, President George W. Bush left his hotel room at the Colony Beach & Tennis Resort in Longboat Key, Florida, where he was on a tour promoting his education policy. Fresh from a run, he rode with a caravan of media and security personnel to the Emma E. Booker Elementary School. On the way there, members of the media overheard radio reports of a "crash." Bush first heard of the attack from senior advisor Karl Rove. Just before he entered the Mrs. Sandra Kay Daniels' second grade classroom, the president spoke over the phone with national security advisor, Condoleezza Rice. She informed him briefly of the first plane hitting the World Trade Center. Bush, still calm and collected, went into the classroom and read with 16 children, joking that they must be sixth graders. At 9:05, chief of staff Andrew Card entered the classroom and whispered the news of the second plane's impact in the president's right ear.

After making brief remarks condemning the attacks, Bush made a hasty departure aboard Air Force One, leaving Florida by 9:55 A.M. For most of the day, the president was shuttled to and from secure locations. Throughout his travels, Bush maintained contact with key advisors. Through these conversations, top leaders down the chain of command devised a first-day strategy of responding to the attacks.

Almost immediately, the nation's infrastructure shut down. Ports and borders were closed, as were all bridges and tunnels into Manhattan. By 9:45 the Federal Aviation Administration had grounded all domestic flights. In another hour, all incoming

President Bush was speaking to a group of schoolchildren in Sarasota, Florida when he heard the news of the second terrorist attack from Chief of Staff Andrew Card. Worried that he might also be a potential target, the president was flown to different locations while accompanied by fighter jets before finally returning to the White House.

international flights were sent to Canada. The United Nations offices in New York were evacuated and Mayor Rudolph Giuliani ordered the evacuation of much of lower Manhattan. New York City mobilized its first responders. More than 40,000 police officers and 11,000 firefighters reported to work. Cameras documented a steady stream of ash-covered people walking north, away from the collapsed towers.

For the first time in history, the Federal Emergency Management Agency deployed nationwide. FEMA is the federal agency charged with coordinating responses to disasters, from floods to terrorist attacks. Mayors and governors ordered the evacuations of the nation's tallest skyscrapers and major landmarks including Walt Disney World, Philadelphia's Liberty Bell and Independence Hall, Seattle's Space Needle and the Gateway Arch in St. Louis.

For the first time in recent memory, the military was called upon to protect the massive geography of the United States. Armed troops patrolled Washington, D.C. Ten military warships, including two aircraft carriers, were deployed along the eastern seaboard. Military aircraft patrolled the airspace over New York and D.C. Governors in New York, New Jersey and Pennsylvania activated the National Guard.

While the country girded itself against new attacks and tried to save lives that were already in danger, the need to protect officials with the authority to lead the nation became an unfortunate reality. Congressional leaders were moved during the day to secure unspecified locations outside D.C. National security adviser Condoleezza Rice and Vice President Dick Cheney stayed in a bunker underneath the White House. Spending much of the day aboard Air Force One, flanked by F-15 fighter jets, President Bush stopped at Air Force bases in Nebraska and Louisiana before returning to the White House in the evening to address the nation from the Oval Office.

As the day faded, attention began to focus on blame and retribution. Who was responsible, Americans asked, and what would be done to pay for the thousands of lost lives? While sources within the military and CIA told newspapers that they believed the attacks were the work of Osama bin Laden, a Saudi Arabia-born terrorist leader with headquarters in

Afghanistan, the government would not officially name bin Laden as the chief suspect.

The rhetoric of war would emerge the next day.

In a September 12 meeting with his National Security Team, President Bush alluded to the coming war: "The deliberate and deadly attacks which were carried out yesterday against our country were more than acts of terror. They were acts of war. This will require our country to unite in steadfast determination and resolve. Freedom and democracy are under attack."

Of the thousands who died on September 11, the toll among uniformed public servants was high: 343 firefighters and paramedics, 23 police officers and 37 Port Authority police officers. About 2,000 children lost a parent, and 50 pregnant women were left without husbands. Thousands of people lost spouses, children, sisters, brothers, and friends. An outpouring of donations came from all over the world. Although funds ebb and flow from distribution and ongoing donation, some striking numbers were reported toward the end of 2001: the American Red Cross raised over $674.4 million, while the September 11th United Way fund raised over $143 million.

In addition, the federal government set up its own September 11th Victim Compensation fund. The fund was the first of its kind ever created in the aftermath of a U.S. disaster. It is estimated that the average benefit would ultimately wind up being about $1.6 million dollars, at a cost to taxpayers of $6 billion.

As the country reeled from the attacks and struggled to make sense of the loss, the government was already taking steps to retaliate against the perpetrators of the attacks and try to safeguard the country from future acts of terrorism. The war on terror would be fought both abroad and at home and would reveal who America could trust to be its allies and enemies.

On the night of September 11, 2001, Americans across the country tuned in to watch President Bush's televised address. His reassuring words of resolve galvanized the nation as he proved himself to be a capable leader in a time of crisis—and soon, in a time of war.

In one of the darker chapters in American history, Japanese-Americans were rounded up and put into internment camps during World War II. After the attacks of September 11, many Arab and South Asian immigrants were also detained in the U.S., which has angered many civil rights groups.

2

A History of Crisis Situations

President Bush and his advisors did not face the task of responding to the attacks empty-handed. They had history as a guide. New plans for disaster response, domestic security and investigation were influenced and colored by the nation's experiences with past national emergencies. From the Japanese raid on Pearl Harbor in 1941 to terrorist attacks in the 1990s, America has learned how to respond to disaster through trial and error.

In the immediate aftermath of September 11, pundits began comparing the tragedy to the Japanese attack on Pearl Harbor in 1941. At the time, the raid on Pearl Harbor was the most deadly foreign attack in U.S. history.

On the morning of December 7, 1941, 353 Japanese aircraft

attacked 100 U.S. ships stationed in Pearl Harbor, Hawaii. The devastation was enormous: 2,403 people died, 188 planes were destroyed, and 8 battleships were damaged or destroyed. President Franklin D. Roosevelt went before Congress the very next day to ask for a declaration of war against Japan. The attack brought America into World War II, fighting with European allies against the united enemy forces of Germany and Japan.

The government's response to the threat of foreign attack in the 1940s has many parallels with its tactics today. There are also several important differences. During World War II and after September 11, the United States government urged citizens to support the war effort by backing their leaders, donating to charity and volunteering their time. During both periods of national crisis, fear about threats from immigrants inspired actions that have been criticized by groups that advocate for individual rights, such as freedom of speech and religion and protection from unreasonable searches and seizures. After the passage of more than half a century, there is a larger consensus condemning the government's actions in the 1940s than its actions in response to the September 11 attacks.

During the 1940s, a growing population of Japanese immigrants had settled on the West Coast. Concern about "enemy aliens" and the loyalties of Japanese-Americans emerged immediately after the attacks. In early 1942, President Franklin D. Roosevelt issued Executive Order 9066, which allowed for the evacuation and incarceration of 120,000 Japanese-Americans. Half of those sent to the so-called internment camps were children; most were U.S. citizens or legal permanent resident aliens. They were held for up to 4 years in remote, heavily fortified camps. They lost their homes and their livelihoods. Some families were separated. Because of poor medical care, some died needlessly.

Military guards killed several interned Japanese who allegedly resisted orders.

The government defended the internment program as necessary protection against the threat of domestic espionage and sabotage. Years later, the Commission on Wartime Relocation and Internment of Civilians, declared that the camps "were motivated largely by racial prejudice, wartime hysteria, and a failure of political leadership." Almost 50 years later, Congress passed the Civil Liberties Act of 1988, which acknowledged that "a grave injustice was done" and mandated Congress to pay each victim of internment $20,000 in reparations. The reparations were sent with a signed apology from the President of the United States on behalf of the American people.

The threat of radical Islamic terrorist campaigns became apparent to many Americans for the first time during the 1990s. Between January and February of 1991, the United States fought an undeclared war with Iraq. The military action, which was set off by Iraq's invasion on neighboring Kuwait in August 1990, was brief and successful. But the war, despite the participation of Middle East nations like Saudi Arabia and Egypt, stirred anti-American sentiments in the Middle East. The reverberations of that animosity weren't felt in the United States until 1993.

That year, on February 26, a bomb exploded in the basement parking garage of the World Trade Center complex. U.S. intelligence officials now believe Osama bin Laden played a large role in planning the attack. Six people died in the blast and more than a thousand were injured. An improvised device made out of fertilizer and compressed hydrogen gas, the bomb produced a 150-foot-wide, five-floor-deep crater. The explosion threatened the stability of World Trade and posed the risk of raw sewage and other hazardous materials leaking into the air and ground water. The New York Fire Department responded with 84 engine companies, 60 truck companies, 28 battalion chiefs, nine deputy chiefs, five rescue companies and 26 other special units, all representing nearly 45 percent of the on-duty staff of the department.

Four terrorists, including the blind cleric, Sheik Omar Abdel Rahman, were convicted in federal court in 1995 of conspiracy to plan the attacks. They were sentenced to 240 years in prison each and fined $250 million. The supposed mastermind of the attacks, Ramzi Yousef, was captured in 1995, convicted in 1997 and sentenced to 240 years in prison.

For Americans, the first World Trade Center bombing was a warning that the kind of violence that plagued Middle East and Ireland could happen here. No more, the public realized, could the bomb blasts and bloodshed be contained within television broadcasts. The attack brought the need for anti-terrorist protection measures into clearer focus than ever before. America's 31,000 local fire departments scrambled to increase disaster response training, and politicians began clamoring for increased spending on domestic security measures.

The next major terrorist attack against the United States occurred on foreign soil. On August 7, 1998, at about 10:40 A.M., a bomb exploded near the U.S. embassy in Nairobi, Kenya. Almost simultaneously, a second bomb was detonated near the embassy in Dar es Salaam, Tanzania. The blasts killed 224 people, twelve of them Americans. More than 5,000 were wounded.

The investigation of the crime scenes, in cooperation with the host countries, revealed a terrorist plot suspected to be the work of Islamic extremists with connections to Osama bin Laden. On May 29, 2001, after over 12 days of deliberations, a Manhattan federal court jury returned a guilty verdict on 302 counts against four men involved in the bombings. Wadih El-Hage, Mohamed Sadeek Odeh,

In recent years, the Middle East has been a breeding ground for anti-American sentiment, with scenes of flag-burning demonstrations becoming almost commonplace to Americans. However, until the World Trade Center bombing of 1993, most Americans felt unaffected by this anger against the U.S.

A Kenyan soldier raises the flag at the American embassy in Nairobi, Kenya, just days after a bomb went off near the embassy on August 7, 1998. A second bomb that detonated near the American embassy in Tanzania killed 224 people and wounded more than 5,000.

Mohamed Rashed Daoud Al-'Owali, and Khalfan Khamis Mohamed were convicted of conspiring with bin Laden and 17 other co-defendants to kill American nationals outside of the United States. Over four months later, in October 2001, they were sentenced to life in federal prison without the possibility of release and ordered to pay a total of $33 million to the U.S. government and individual victims of the bombings.

Thirteen of the 22 defendants in embassy bombings, including bin Laden, remain at large, although they were indicted in 1998. The Saudi exile also is suspected of playing a large role in the attack on the U.S.S. *Cole* in the Yemeni port of Aden in October 2000, which killed 17 soldiers.

President Bush and his National Security Council would soon become household faces as they regularly appeared on TV shows and in press conferences updating the American public on various aspects of the war on terror.

3

The Key Players

W hen America is plunged into chaos or faces a serious threat, major government agencies responsible for investigation, disaster response, public health and safety are mobilized. These agencies, including the FBI, the CIA and FEMA, were created to respond to perceived threats, and change each time those threats are realized. In light of new facts of life since September 11 attacks, the offices may have to evolve again.

The Federal Bureau of Investigation (FBI) grew out of a small, unnamed force of agents appointed in 1908 by Attorney General Charles J. Bonaparte. Now the main investigative arm of the United States Department of Justice, the FBI investigates major crimes and assists law enforcement agencies in states and municipalities. In addition, the bureau is charged with protecting the

United States from foreign intelligence and terrorist activities.

The FBI director is appointed by the president and confirmed by the Senate for a term of up to ten years. As of January 31, 2002, the FBI had approximately 11,000 Special Agents and 16,000 Professional Support Personnel. The FBI has played a key role in investigating the terrorist attacks and the deadly mailing of letters laced with anthrax during the fall of 2001.

Created by act of Congress in 1947, to replace the wartime Office of Strategic Services, the Central Intelligence Agency (CIA) is the main intelligence-gathering arm of the executive branch. In layman's terms, the CIA is the spy agency. Responsible for gathering foreign information relevant to national security, much of what happens within the CIA is kept secret: the agency can keep the size of its staff secret and spend funds without telling the public where the money goes. However, the CIA is prohibited from investigating U.S. citizens. The CIA's responsibilities in investigating terrorism center on collecting information on the convert actions of terrorist groups. The Director of Central Intelligence, the chief of the CIA, is also responsible for coordinating intelligence gathering by other agencies, such as the State Department and the Defense Department.

The CIA was criticized in the fall of 2001 for failing to intercept and disrupt plans for the attacks. CIA director George Tenet said his agency had been "at war" with bin Laden for more than five years. Critics said the CIA failed because it didn't have strong enough capabilities in human intelligence, the personal connections through which spies ferret out covert plans.

The Federal Emergency Management Agency (FEMA), founded in 1979, is an independent government agency charged with responding to disaster, from floods to tornadoes, hurricanes, earthquakes, hazardous spills and fires, and even acts of terrorism. The agency also has the task of planning for and helping prevent such tragedies. Working with the newly formed Office of Homeland Security, FEMA's Office of National Preparedness was given responsibility for helping to ensure that the nation's first responders were trained and equipped to deal with weapons of mass destruction.

The Centers for Disease Control and Prevention (CDC) is responsible for protecting the health and safety of Americans both at home and abroad. The CDC directs national efforts in disease prevention and control and environmental health. Located in Atlanta, Georgia, the CDC, is part of the Department of Health and Human Services. The CDC was called upon in the late fall of 2001, when 23 people were sickened by letters laced with anthrax, a deadly and contagious bacteria.

The government's response to a breach of national security is never the job of the president alone. Cabinet members and key advisors assist the president, contributing specialized knowledge and skills to create a plan that spans from providing food to rescue workers to coordinating a military attack. Congressional leaders also impact national strategy by voting on the laws that fund and detail the nation's actions.

The attacks tested of the abilities of a green administration. George W. Bush came to the White House in January 2001 from the Texas statehouse. He had little experience in foreign policy. The son of President George Herbert Walker Bush, George W. Bush had worked in the oil business and co-owned a baseball team before becoming governor of the largest state in the union. He campaigned on his trademark "compassionate conservatism," a brand of right-wing thinking that emphasizes programs designed to help the less-advantaged improve their lives on their own, without direct government support.

Some critics said the president floundered immediately after attacks, and scolded him for using harsh, militaristic language. But as the weeks wore on, conservative and liberal observers alike agreed that the president had matured quickly as he raced to lead a nation in crisis. With a congress eager to smooth the legislative process in a time of war, Bush received wide support for his military, diplomatic and domestic proposals.

For the American public, Bush defined the war in black and white. Freedom, he said, was at war with fear. In promoting his policies for homeland security and his aims abroad, the president sent the same message: the American way had to be protected. In a September 20 speech before a joint session of Congress, he reiterated that theme. "On September the 11th, enemies of freedom committed an act of war against our country. Americans have known wars—but for the past 136 years, they have been wars on foreign soil, except for one Sunday in 1941. Americans have known the casualties of war—but not at the center of a great city on a peaceful morning. Americans have known surprise attacks—but never before on thousands of civilians. All of this was brought upon us in a single day—and night fell on a different world, a world where freedom itself is under attack."

Attorney General John Ashcroft, a former Missouri governor and senator, became a powerful player in domestic security after September 11. Public alerts about the threat of new attacks came from him, not from the Office of Homeland Security. As the United States' chief prosecutor and head of the Department of Justice, Ashcroft oversaw the investigation into the attacks and criminal prosecution of suspects involved. So far, only one terrorist has been brought to trial in connection with the violence of September 11. On December the 11th, 2001, a grand jury in Alexandria, Virginia, indicted Zacarias Moussaoui and charged him with six different conspiracy offenses. The Department of Justice is seeking the death penalty.

Ashcroft, a conservative Republican, has said that his role in the war on terrorism is designed to be preventative as well as punitive. He oversaw the detention of hundreds of foreign citizen, most of Arab or South Asian descent, and the prosecution of alleged terrorists. He allowed investigators to monitor

Attorney General John Ashcroft's aggressive stance on domestic security has met with sharp criticism with many who argue that some of his tactics, come at the price of basic civil rights and constitutional freedoms.

privileged communications between the detainees and their lawyers and ordered the questioning of more than 5,000 men, most of Middle Eastern descent.

A tenured professor of political science at Stanford University, National Security Advisor Condoleezza Rice is a

National Security Advisor Condoleezza Rice has considerable experience in foreign affairs, and has been instrumental in shaping the Bush administration's foreign policy. Additionally, she has appeared on the Arabic cable news channel Al-Jazeera to try and bolster support for the war on terror.

specialist on Russia and arms control. She served in the first Bush administration as an advisor on Soviet and East European affairs. Rice makes recommendations to Bush and his National Security Council on issues of defense and security.

Secretary of State Colin Powell, the highest ranking African-American in the U.S. government, was raised in the Bronx, N.Y. In his 35 years of Army service, Powell rose to the rank of 4-star General. From October 1, 1989 to September 30, 1993, he served as Chairman of the Joint Chiefs of Staff, the highest military position in the Department of Defense. He oversaw 28 missions, including Operation Desert Storm in the 1991 Persian Gulf War. In his newest post, as secretary of state, Powell is the president's chief foreign policy advisor and heads the agency charged with leading the United States' interactions with other nations.

Secretary of Defense Donald Rumsfeld came to the Bush

administration with decades of political service under his belt. He had served in the Nixon and Ford administrations, as an advisor and under Ford, as Secretary of Defense. The bespectacled veteran's leadership style, often described as caustic, has served him well in guiding the military response to the terrorist attacks. Instead of being derided as pushy and aggressive, he is seen now as blunt and honest, qualities of value during trying times. Rumsfeld will also oversee the prosecution in military tribunals of perhaps hundreds of suspected terrorists.

In the wake of the attacks, Rumsfeld lobbied for reforms that would transform the American military from a slow-moving giant into a lithe, quick responder. "Even as we prosecute this war on terrorism, we must be preparing for the next war," he said. "We have to begin shifting the balance in our arsenal between manned and unmanned capabilities, between short- and long-range systems, stealthy and non-stealthy systems, between shooters and sensors, and between vulnerable and hardened systems."

Vice President Dick Cheney took a quiet role in the first months after the attacks. In fact, on several occasions, he was moved to secure, unnamed locations during security threats. Nonetheless, Cheney was valued as a source of institutional memory and traditional Washington leadership savvy among the younger officials in the Bush administration. Cheney served as defense secretary to the elder Bush and worked as a key advisor to presidents Gerald Ford and Richard Nixon.

On September 20, the president created the office of Homeland Security and named Pennsylvania Governor Tom Ridge director. The president envisioned an office that would "develop and coordinate a comprehensive national strategy to strengthen protections against terrorist threats or attacks in the United States." Governor Ridge, a Republican, was elected twice to the top post in Pennsylvania. He left before the end of his second term to direct the office of Homeland Security.

For the American public, one of the more reassuring aspects of Operation Enduring Freedom was the relatively low number of U.S. casualties suffered initially. Additionally, the Bush administration worked to build an international coalition who also supported the war on terror.

4

Support for the War on Terror

From the start, President Bush sought to build a broad international coalition to support his military and diplomatic efforts. In addition to relying heavily on traditional allies in Europe, the administration reached out to friends in the Middle East and even to countries with rocky diplomatic histories with the United States.

President Bush called British Prime Minister Tony Blair, a close friend, at 7:30 A.M. on September 12. Blair pledged his support. He agreed that Bush needed to reach out to multi-national organizations, such as the United Nations and the members of the North Atlantic Treaty Organization, to facilitate alliances and build the framework for a military attack.

Egyptian President Hosni Mubarak, a longtime U.S. ally,

denounced the attacks immediately. Having struggled with terrorism over the last decade, his administration endorsed much of the U.S. response to September 11, including the war in Afghanistan.

One of the first nations to hear the United State's call for support was Pakistan. The Muslim nation borders Afghanistan and was crucial to American strategic plans. Pakistani leaders heard an ultimatum that reverberated across the Middle East and South East Asia: "We're in a different world now," Bush said. "You're either with us or against us." His message was clear: any nations that refused to aid U.S. war efforts would risk attack themselves. Pakistan acceded to U.S. demands and became a major staging area for the air war. Pakistani President Pervez Musharraf, a general who took power in a 1999 coup, allowed U.S. and British warplanes to use Pakistani airspace, donated two Pakistani airfields, shared intelligence about suspected terrorists, and cooperated with the FBI to capture suspected al-Qaeda and Taliban fugitives in northern Pakistan. In the spring of 2002, American and Pakistani troops made cooperative raids on the tribal regions near the Afghan-Pakistani border, searching for the last al-Qaeda and Taliban holdouts. While the U.S. relied on Pakistan as an ally, the nation has also been charged with promoting terrorism. Pakistan's intelligence services—known as the Interservices Intelligence, or ISI—have provided covert but well-documented support to terrorist groups fighting against India in the disputed territory of Kashmir. In addition, the United States also reached out to the Northern Alliance, a loose coalition of tribes that have been fighting the Taliban.

Russia, once the United State's enemy, proved invaluable in the task of planning military strikes. Once engaged in a 10-year war with Afghanistan, Russian military officials understood

In addition to conventional warfare in Afghanistan, the U.S. military also dropped leaflets offering a reward for Osama bin Laden and Ayman Al-Zawahiri. Other leaflets reassured the Afghan people that the U.S. were not targeting them but the Taliban and al-Qaeda.

how to fight in the mountainous, rocky terrain, and how to root fighters out of hiding places in numerous caves.

U.S. military strategists, guided by Secretary of Defense Donald Rumsfeld and Army General Tommy R. Franks, outlined an assault built around pinpoint air strikes and covert missions by Special Forces. The capture of Osama bin Laden was considered of almost equal importance as a goal as the end of Taliban rule in Afghanistan. Bin Laden, a 44-year-old Saudi exile and millionaire, may be the world's most notorious fugitive. He founded and leads the al-Qaeda terrorist network. The son of a wealthy building contractor, bin Laden dedicated his life to Islam as a youth and used his inheritance—estimated at $80 million to $300 million—to pay for terrorist activities against the United States.

The military response to the terrorist attacks began on October 7, 2001. British and American planes attacked Kabul, one of the main Taliban strongholds. At the same time, allied forces began dropping food and medical packages for Afghanistan's impoverished citizens. Military aircraft also dropped rafts of leaflets pledging friendship with the Afghan people and condemning the oppressive rule of the Taliban. Reminders of the $25 million dollar bounty on Osama bin Laden were part of the leaflet drop.

Additionally, Rumsfeld and Rice took the extraordinary step of appearing on Al-Jazeera, the Arab news channel, in hopes of gaining sympathy or understanding for the war on terror. Al-Jazeera, a channel that likens itself as CNN's equivalent in the Arab world, won notoriety for broadcasting videotaped messages from bin Laden himself. The Bush administration knew that reaching Muslim audiences—whose anti-U.S. feelings were only worsening in reaction to the war in Afghanistan—would require careful public relations work. Former U.S. ambassador to Syria Christopher Ross, who is fluent in Arabic, also appeared on Al-Jazeera to comment on one of bin Laden's videotaped messages.

On November 10, the Northern Alliance seized the key northern city Mazar-i-Sharif, its way cleared by U.S. bombing raids. Only two days later, Kabul was taken by the Northern Alliance with no resistance from Taliban forces. Women, who had largely been forced to stay indoors, walked the streets. Men cut their beards, which was also in opposition to Taliban law. Only a few weeks later, however, the victorious mood was tempered by the first American combat death. A CIA agent by the name of Mike Spann was beaten to death in an uprising of Taliban prisoners near the captured city of Mazar-i-Sharif. In another shocking turn of events, the American public came to learn that only hours before his death, Mr. Spann was interviewing a Taliban prisoner distinguished by the fact that he was American. John Walker Lindh was a California native who had come to Afghanistan to study Islam and joined the Taliban. Lindh was indicted by an Alexandria, Va., federal grand jury in January. He was charged with aiding terrorist organizations and conspiracy to kill Americans. If convicted, he may face up to three life sentences plus an additional 90 years.

By the first week of December, the Taliban surrendered Kandahar, its last stronghold. Later that month, the leader of a new, interim Afghan government was appointed. Four Afghan factions in an accord brokered by the United Nations chose Hamid Karzai. Osama bin Laden and Mullah Muhammad Omar were still at large.

During the offensive strikes in Afghanistan, U.S. forces captured hundreds of Taliban and al-Qaeda fighters. The United States questioned the detainees and transferred them to U.S. detention facilities near the former Taliban stronghold of Kandahar and to Navy ships in the Indian Ocean. In January 2002, the military began transferring the detainees to Camp X-Ray at the U.S. naval base in Guantanamo Bay, Cuba. Some civil rights groups have lashed out at the military for holding the detainees under what they claim to be inhumane conditions. Government officials defend the conditions at Camp X-Ray and say the fighters have provided information on new attacks that may have saved American lives.

Detainees from Operation Enduring Freedom were flown to Camp X-Ray in Guantanamo Bay, Cuba where they were held for questioning. Civil rights groups have called the detainees' conditions inhumane, a charge the government has denied.

American military forces will remain in Afghanistan for many months, ensuring the success of the new government and helping to train a new military. As of May, many Taliban and al-Qaeda fighters still resisted surrender. In this war against terrorism, a definitive peace may prove elusive. Unlike World Wars I and II, when we fought against an enemy state, this war pits the free world against a villain that knows no borders and defies statehood.

Homeland Security Director Tom Ridge introduced a new color-coded warning system to the American public in order to differntiate between levels of severity of terror alerts. This move came in response to criticism over vague terror alerts previously issued by the government.

5

Domestic Security

The most visible part of the government's response to terrorism is domestic security. From police patrolling city streets to baggage screeners in airports, the people and systems that guard us are a common, everyday sight. After September 11, the measures designed to protect Americans became even more prominent. F-15 Eagle fighter jets cruised over major cities. Hundreds of National Guard troops were stationed at airports and more than 1,600 were deployed along U.S. borders with Mexico and Canada. In the nation's capital, armored tanks patrolled the streets.

But these steps were just temporary safeguards. In the months following September 11, government officials sought to establish permanent protections against attacks on home soil. The results of their efforts were new government agencies, tougher restrictions for immigrants, an increased police and military presence, new legislation governing aviation security and a higher level of screening for mail passing through the post office.

Not surprisingly, concerns about domestic security made it easier to pass legislation to increase spending. The Bush administration's proposed budget for 2003 would raise defense spending by $45 billion, or 13 percent, and double money spent on homeland defense to $36 billion—including $11 billion for border security and $5.9 billion for combating bioterrorism.

In his State of the Union address on January 29, 2002, Bush argued that the increased spending would build protections against other threats in addition to terrorism, saying, "Homeland security will make America not only stronger, but, in many ways, better. Knowledge gained from bioterrorism research will improve public health. Stronger police and fire departments will mean safer neighborhoods. Stricter border enforcement will help combat illegal drugs. And as government works to better secure our homeland, America will continue to depend on the eyes and ears of alert citizens."

Hoping to help unite the various agencies involved in protecting domestic security, President Bush signed an executive order opening the Office of Homeland Security less than two weeks after September 11. The office serves only as an advisor to other agencies, and lacks the power to direct their actions. Some policy makers complained that the office lacked the power to force real change. In 2002, the Bush administration approached Congress with a plan to create a cabinet-level agency.

In March, the Office of Homeland Security unveiled a five-tier national alert system designed to inform the public of the risk of attacks. The color-coded rankings rise in order of "threat conditions" from low (green), to guarded (blue), elevated (yellow), high (orange), and severe (red). "Even in a low level of risk, there's a recognition that the possibility or the potential of a terrorist attack still exists in the world today," Ridge said. "And

One of the stepped-up security measures planned for airports included having air marshals onboard flights. Here a group of air marshals perform tactical training inside a retired airplane.

that, I think, is a permanent condition in the world. Whether or not we ever get to low, I'm hopeful, but I still think it's years away."

The Homeland Security Council, established by the same order that created the Office of Homeland Security, brings together senior officials to discuss security policies that fall outside the jurisdictions of any one agency. Along with Ridge, the council includes the president and vice president; the secretaries of defense, health and human services, transportation, and the treasury; the attorney general and the directors of the FBI and the CIA.

Perhaps the most urgent security concern on the part of the American public after September 11 was the safety of air travel. In November, Congress passed the Aviation and Transportation Security Act. The wide-ranging measure was designed to improve security on airplanes and in airports and established a new administration for transportation security within the Department of Transportation. The Transportation Security

Administration directs security measures for all modes of transportation, including aviation, rail, bus, and commercial shipping, as well as ports. The act also required federal employees to perform all security checks at U.S. airports within a year. It called for about 30,000 English-speaking baggage screeners to assume the duty of inspecting luggage at more than 400 airports. In the past, only a small portion of luggage was screened by bomb detection systems; the new law required all luggage to go through screening by January 2002. The legislation called for an increase in the number of sky marshals aboard planes and provided funding to help airliners pay for security improvements, like fortified cockpit doors and training for flight crews. A new system was created allowing passenger names to be compared with law enforcement "watch lists."

"The federal government will set high standards, and we will enforce them," Bush said at a signing ceremony at Reagan National Airport. "These have been difficult days for Americans who fly and for American aviation. A proud industry has been hit hard. But this nation has seen the dedication and spirit of our pilots and flight crews, and the hundreds of thousands of hard-working people who keep America flying. We know they will endure."

In the immediate aftermath of the attacks, the government ordered stopgap safeguards that are still subject to change. It limited carry-on luggage to one bag and one personal item, permitted only ticketed passengers beyond gates, banned knives and box cutters, and instituted random searches of passengers and their carry-on luggage at the gates. Curbside check-in was forbidden—except for airlines that could provide the same level of security and screening on the street as at the ticket counter.

Airlines were desperately dependent upon government funding for the new security measures: the industry itself was facing financial ruin. In the public panic following the attacks, air traffic dropped precipitously. The attacks resulted in the first total shutdown of air travel in United States history. Some airports like Washington's Reagan National, due to its proximity to the White House and the Pentagon, remained closed longer than airports in other major cities. Aviation insurers promised to raise their rates. On September 21, Congress overwhelmingly approved a $15 billion industry bailout package to help the airlines recover. The package included $5 billion in cash payments to compensate the airlines for their losses during the two days when the government shut down air travel immediately after the attacks and up to $10 billion in loan guarantees.

Just weeks after Americans were forced to begin thinking of airplanes as weapons of mass destruction, a new specter of terror emerged. Letters laced with anthrax were mailed to media outlets and politicians in the first fatal instance of biological terrorism on U.S. soil. Human anthrax has three major clinical forms: cutaneous, inhalation, and gastrointestinal. If left untreated, all forms can lead to death.

The contaminated letters infected 23 people, killing five of them. Contaminated letters sent to the *New York Post* and NBC's Tom Brokaw had a September 18, 2001 postmark. Letters postmarked October 9 were sent to senators Tom Daschle and Patrick Leahy—these carried a more potent form of anthrax. Officials believe contaminated letters were also sent to American Media, in Florida, and the New York offices of CBS and ABC, where there were also confirmed cases of anthrax. The mailings crippled the postal system in the northeastern United States, spawning hoaxes and hysteria over any white powder. Investigators believe the bacteria were spread by a domestic terrorist. The U.S. Postal Service has begun irradiating some "targeted" mail to destroy any possible bacteria.

The government's efforts to build a new strategy for

REWARD
UP TO $2,500,000

For information leading to the arrest and conviction of the individual(s) responsible for the mailing of letters containing anthrax to the New York Post, Tom Brokaw at NBC, Senator Tom Daschle and Senator Patrick Leahy:

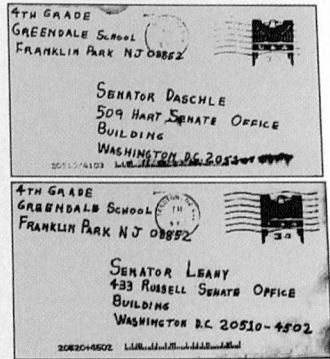

AS A RESULT OF EXPOSURE TO ANTHRAX, FIVE (5) PEOPLE HAVE DIED.

The person responsible for these deaths...

- Likely has a scientific background/work history which may include a specific familiarity with anthrax

- Has a level of comfort in and around the Trenton, NJ area due to present or prior association

Anyone having information, contact **America's Most Wanted** at **1-800-CRIME TV** or the **FBI** via e-mail at amerithrax@fbi.gov

All information will be held in strict confidence. Reward payment will be made in accordance with the conditions of Postal Service Reward Notice 296, dated February 2000. Source of reward funds: US Postal Service and FBI $2,000,000; ADVO, Inc. $500,000.

AMERICA FIGHTS BAC

In the fall of 2001, the nation reeled in shock yet again as mysterious letters tainted with anthrax spores began appearing in different locations in the US. The letters killed five people and sparked fear and paranoia into many, inspiring hoax letters and many false alarms.

domestic security exposed problems with the old system. Much of the criticism fell on the Immigration and Naturalization Service, an agency of the Department of Justice responsible for regulating the admission of foreign-born people into the United States and administering benefits to new immigrants.

The INS works with Customs Service to secure U.S. borders, and is thus given some of the blame for allowing terrorists to enter the county. Months after the attacks took place, the INS delivered student visas, or entry permits, to the flight school where several of them trained. The snafu was seen as a painful reminder of the service's problems with paperwork. The 19 September 11 hijackers entered the United States on legal visas, although three had expired visas.

Immediately following the September 11 attacks, border traffic came to a near halt as the nation went on highest possible alert. After the first few weeks, long delays at the border were cut as the agencies shifted resources, asked agents to work longer hours, and staffed border crossings with National Guardsmen. Homeland Security Director Tom Ridge and senior Customs Service and INS officials have met with their counterparts in Mexico and Canada about ways to guard U.S. borders more effectively without disrupting trade.

The investigation into the attacks also shed light on the importance of safeguarding government officials when military and political power centers become targets. On September 11, the Bush administration began rotating key civilian officials through secret East Coast locations, thus ensuring the presence of people with knowledge and power should an attack devastate the capital. This so-called "shadow government" is outlined in an Eisenhower era measure, the "Continuity of Operations Plan," designed to safeguard federal rule. About 100 managers who report for "Bunker Duty" stay below ground 24 hours a day for periods of about 90 days in two secret locations. The Cold War Era plan was never activated during the decades of tension with the Soviet Union.

On October 26, 2001, President Bush signed the Patriot Act into law which allowed the police and other agencies greater authority to search homes and property and eavesdrop on communications.

Ongoing Efforts

Since the attacks on America in 2001, the Bush administration repeatedly stated that its main priority was the destruction of terrorism. That goal would be realized, the president said, not only with air raids on the caves and mountains of Afghanistan, but with legislation and policy aimed at prosecuting terrorists, investigating and uncovering their plans and actions and eliminating their sources of funding.

The government wanted to investigate and prosecute the attackers themselves, a task that, despite its global scope, began with simple police work. The search for clues began immediately after the attacks of September 11. Hundreds of FBI agents and police fanned out across the flashpoints of the attacks: Boston's Logan airport, where two of the planes took off; Washington

D.C.'s Reagan International Airport; and a flight-training school in Florida where some of the hijackers had trained. Hundreds of CIA operatives were dispatched to Afghanistan. As investigators collected evidence, congress began developing ways to strengthen the government's ability to conduct surveillance, hold suspects and gather intelligence.

In late October, Congress passed the U.S.A. Patriot Act, a sweeping anti-terrorism bill designed to strengthen the government's ability to uncover covert terrorist operations. The law greatly increased the Federal Bureau of Investigation's power to collect domestic intelligence. Historically, the FBI has concentrated on solving major crimes. The Patriot Act gave the bureau greater authority to collect information, through wire taps and searches. The law also gave the CIA increased access to information gathered by federal grand juries, whose inquiries and evidence are usually kept secret.

Since September, the Justice Department has detained more than 1,200 foreign nationals, mostly men of Arab and South Asian descent. The Patriot Act made such detentions much easier. Most of the men are being held for immigration violations or minor crimes. Some were held as material witnesses. The Justice Department withheld the names of the detainees and kept secret the details of individual cases. An internal review is underway to determine whether the department has violated the civil liberties of men in custody.

In November, Attorney General Ashcroft announced a program giving prospective immigrants the option of trading "useful and reliable" information on terrorists for citizenship and other incentives. Ashcroft has defended the bold steps taken to detain and prosecute terrorists saying, "To those who scare peace-loving people with phantoms of lost liberty, my message is this: Your tactics only aid terrorists, for they erode our national unity and diminish our resolve. They give ammunition to . . . enemies and pause to . . . friends."

Many Democrats in congress railed against Ashcroft's accusations that criticizing the Justice Department equaled supporting terrorism. "This is not a question of whether you are for or against terrorists," said Judiciary Committee Chairman Patrick J. Leahy, a Democrat from Vermont who was a staunch critic of the administration's anti-terrorism efforts. "Everyone is against terrorists. This is about whether we are adequately protecting civil liberties."

Many people argued that the Patriot Act would set a dangerous precedent, and erase protections for all Americans built up during the 20th century campaign to limit the government's ability to perform searches and seizures. "The bill enters new and uncharted territory by breaking down traditional barriers between law enforcement and foreign intelligence," Leahy said.

The first charges related to the terrorist attacks were filed against Zacarias Moussaoui, a French citizen of Moroccan descent, when he was indicted in December 2001. Prosecutors believe Moussaoui, who is charged with conspiracy to commit terrorism, was supposed to be the 20th hijacker. Some foreign citizens prosecuted in connection with the attacks may be tried before military tribunals. Bush issued an executive order in November allowing trials before these special military courts which have different standards for evidence, conviction, sentencing and appeal than civilian courts. Defendants in military tribunals face juries of military officers and can be confronted with kinds of evidence, such as hearsay and second hand evidence, that are not allowed in civilian courts.

Part of the government's plan to block terrorism is financial. A section of the U.S.A. Patriot Act, the International Money Laundering Abatement and Financial Anti-Terrorism Act of 2001, is aimed at blocking terror funding. The bill increases the authority of the president and Treasury Department to block suspects' assets and seize records. The law may restrict or block

A courtroom drawing of Zacarias Moussaoui, who is the only person charged with direct involvement with the September 11 terrorist attacks. He was allegedly the 20th hijacker among the four teams of hijackers.

certain foreign groups linked to terror or money laundering from accessing the U.S. financial system. It forces monetary institutions to close accounts maintained by foreign "shell banks"—entities without real customers that often serve as fronts for tax evasion and money laundering. The act also facilitates information-sharing between financial institutions and the federal government. Finally, it charges the Treasury Department with building a database of financial intelligence that can be accessed by the CIA.

In the hopes of coordinating the resources of agencies with financial expertise, the Bush administration set up Operation Green Quest and the Foreign Terrorist Asset Tracking Center. These groups, composed of experts from agencies such as the Customs Service and the Internal Revenue Service, led to several arrests and asset seizures. "The first strike in the war against terror targeted the terrorists' financial support," Bush said during a speech on November 7, 2001 at the Financial Crime Enforcement Network in Vienna, Virginia. "We put the world's financial institutions on notice: if you do business with terrorists, if you support them or sponsor them, you will not do business with the United States of America."

In November 2001, federal officials raided al-Barakaat, a Somalia-based financial institution with offices in the United States and 40 other nations. The Bush administration alleged that al-Barakaat helped finance terrorist groups worldwide, including al-Qaeda. Federal agents armed with warrants searched al-Barakaat offices in Massachusetts, Ohio, and Virginia; shut down eight al-Barakaat offices; and froze $1.9 million in assets. Experts say al-Barakaat may have provided $15 to $20 per year to terrorist organizations, out of a total of $300–$400 that passed through the business's coffers.

The government imposed tougher reporting requirements on financial institutions, created new multi-agency investigative units to track down terrorists' assets and transmission channels, blocked bank accounts, and persuaded many other countries to identify and block terrorist funds at home. The United States and other countries had frozen more than $80 million in terrorist-related assets as of January 2002. More than 145 countries and jurisdictions have placed blocks on terrorist assets.

Depending on how U.S. courts rule on challenges to the Patriot Act, the powers of law enforcement agencies may grow dramatically. Legal experts say the law erodes civil liberties protections and governmental limitations built up over the last 25 years. U.S. courts have already begun to redefine the legal parameters of the war on terrorism. In a decision that challenges the Justice Department's handling of detainees being held in the United States, a federal court judge in May ruled against jailing material witnesses so that they might testify in grand jury investigations. The Justice Department has jailed dozens of such witnesses since September 11, and Attorney General John Ashcroft suggested that the department might appeal.

From the start, Bush emphasized that he was waging a war against terrorism, not against Islam or the people of Afghanistan. To help drive home this point, the United States coupled military raids with humanitarian efforts of unprecedented scale. Through aide workers on the ground and aerial drops, more than 370,000 tons of food have been delivered to Afghanistan's six million hungry citizens. Aide workers are working with local farmers to help revive agricultural industries, which once accounted for more than 80 percent of the nation's business. Doctors and nurses are being trained and hospitals repaired and restocked with new supplies. A campaign is underway to vaccinate 9 million children against measles—the cause of 40 percent of the country's childhood deaths. Mine-clearing experts are working to restore access to many parts of the country.

Secretary of State Colin Powell, whose job demands he represent the United States to the rest of the world, stressed the importance of rebuilding Afghanistan in a speech at the McConnell Center for Political Leadership at the University of Louisville in November 2001. "Compare the Taliban's depredations with the response of the international community to the plight of the Afghan people. We are feeding millions of Afghans put at risk by drought, famine and Taliban misrule. . . . We should be proud that the United States, our country, is the largest contributor to this effort to help the desperate Afghan people, and we will do more. . . . One message that leaps out from the events of September 11th is very clear. American leadership in foreign affairs has never been more important. And job one for American leadership in this period is the fight against terrorists."

To reinforce the notion that the U.S. was at war with terrorism and not Afghanistan itself, President Bush called for American children to donate $1 each toward the America's Fund for Afghan Children. The U.S. military has also made many food drops on Afghanistan as well.

Clearly, the war on terror is going to continue for an indefinite amount of time and test the mettle of the government and the American people. It will be up to the leaders to guide the rest of the country through these uncertain times while also being careful to remain in good stead with the global community. While America may never again know the sense of security and peace that it knew before the attacks of September 11, it will be up to the government to try and thwart another attack and ensure that terrorist networks worldwide are disrupted.

http://911digitalarchive.org/websites/content/essays
   [Personal experiences and accounts from September 11, 2001]

http://www.lib.umich.edu/govdocs/usterror.html#terrfin
   [University of Michigan Documents Center]

Council on Foreign Relations

1779 Massachusetts
Avenue, N.W.
Washington, DC 20036
Tel. (202) 518-3400
Fax (202) 986-2984

The Harold Pratt House

58 East 68th Street
New York, NY 10021
Tel. (212) 434-9400
Fax: (212) 434-9800
http://www.cfr.org

White House

1600 Pennsylvania Avenue NW
Washington, DC 20500
http://www.whitehouse.gov

Federal Aviation Administration

800 Independence Avenue, S.W., Room 810
Washington, DC 20591
http://www.faa.gov

Stevens, Paul Schott. *U.S. Armed Forces and Homeland Defense:
The Legal Framework.* Washington, DC: CSIS Publications, 2001.

Coredesman, Anthony H. and Justin G. *Cyber-Threats, Information
Welfare, and Critical Infrastructure Protection: Defending the
U.S. Homeland.* Westport, Conn.: Praeger Pub Text, 2001.

Editors of *Life Magazine. One Nation: America Remembers
September 11, 2001.* New York: Little Brown & Company, 2001.

Lee, Jenniffer. *100 Ways to Strengthen & Unify Our Country.*
West Palm Beach, Fla.: Aribet Books, 2001.

Associated Press, September 11, 2001. "POOL REPORTS 1—3."

Balz, Dan and Woodward, Bob. "America's Chaotic Road to War." *The Washington Post*, January 27, 2002.

Balz, Dan and Woodward, Bob. "'We Will Rally the World' Bush and his Advisers Set Objectives, but Struggled With How to Achieve Them." *The Washington Post*, January 28, 2002.

Bridis, Ted and Neil Jr. "FBI system covertly searches e-mail." *The Wall Street Journal Online*. July 20, 2000.

Bush, George. Speech. Financial Crime Enforcement Network in Vienna, Va. November 7, 2001.

Bush, George. Speech. The President's State of the Union Address. The United States Capitol, Washington, D.C. January 29, 2002.

Eggen, Dan. "Ashcroft Defends Anti-Terrorism Steps." *Washington Post*, December 7, 2001.

Eilperin, Juliet. "House Ponders Issues of Governance After Catastrophe." *The Washington Post*, March 8, 2002.

Karon, Tony. "The War For Muslim Hearts And Minds." *Time*, November 9, 2001.

McGee, Jim. "An Intelligence Giant in the Making." *Washington Post*, November 4, 2001.

Miller, Bill. "National Alert System Defines Five Shades of Terrorist Threat." *Washington Post*, March 13, 2002

Powell, Colin. Speech. McConnell Center for Political Leadership, University of Louisville, Kentucky. November 19, 2001

Ricks, Thomas E. "Rumsfeld Cites Terrorism in New Call for Military Reform." *The Washington Post*, February 1, 2002.

The New York Times, October 14, 2001. "A NATION CHALLENGED: The Hunted: The 22 Most Wanted Suspects, in a Five-Act Drama of Global Terror."

Afghanistan war, 33-37, 39
  and al-Qaeda, 35, 36, 37, 39
  and American combat deaths, 37
  and Bush, 14, 27-28, 33-36
  and detainees, 37
  and humanitarian efforts, 54
  international support for, 33-35, 36
  military phase of, 35-36, 37, 39
  and new Afghanistan government, 37
  and Northern Alliance, 34, 36
  and public relations efforts, 36
  and Taliban, 34, 36, 37, 39, 54
Air travel, security of, 11-12, 43-45
Al-Barakaat, 53
Al-Jazeera, 37
Al-Qaeda, 34, 36, 37, 39, 53
Anthrax, 26, 27, 45
Ashcroft, John, 28-29, 50-51, 54
Aviation and Transportation Security
  Act, 43-44

Bin Laden, Osama, 13-14, 20, 22-23,
  26, 35-36
Bioterrorism
  and anthrax, 26, 27, 45
  budget for, 42
Blair, Tony, 33
Borders, and domestic security, 47
Britain, and Afghanistan war, 33, 34
Bush, George W.
  and advisors, 11, 13, 29-31
  and Afghanistan war, 14, 27-28,
    33-35
  and cabinet, 27, 28-31
  and domestic security, 42, 44
  and financial support of terrorists,
    52-53
  and humanitarian efforts in
    Afghanistan, 54
  security of, 11, 13
  and September 11 attacks, 11, 27-28
  and war on terrorism, 49

Cabinet, 27, 28-31
Camp X-Ray (Cuba), 37
Card, Andrew, 11
Centers for Disease Control and
  Prevention (CDC), 27

Central Intelligence Agency (CIA), 13,
  26, 31, 52
Cheney, Dick, 13, 31
Civil Liberties Act of 1988, 19
Cole, USS, 23
Congress, 19, 43-44, 45, 50-51, 53
Courts, 50-51, 53-54
Cuba, detainees in, 37
Customs Service, 47, 52

Domestic security, 41-47
  and air travel, 43-45
  an Congress, 27
  and anthrax, 26, 27, 45
  and Attorney General, 28-29
  and Bush, 42, 44
  and cabinet, 27, 28-31
  and CDC, 27
  and CIA, 25-26
  and FBI, 25-26, 34
  and FEMA, 26-27
  for government officials, 11, 13, 47
  and immigration, 46-47, 50
  and National Security Advisor, 11,
    13, 29-30
  and Office of Homeland Security,
    26-27, 28, 31, 42-43

Egypt, and Afghanistan war, 33-34
Embassy bombings, 20, 22-23

Federal Aviation Administration, 10,
  11-12
Federal Bureau of Investigation (FBI),
  25-26, 34, 50
Federal Emergency Management
  Agency (FEMA), 13, 26-27
Foreign Terrorist Asset Tracking
  Center, 52
Franks, Tommy R., 35

Giuliani, Rudolph, 12

Homeland Security Council, 43
Homeland Security, Office of, 26-27,
  28, 31, 42-43

Immigration, and terrorism, 46-47, 50

Immigration and Naturalization
Service, 46-47
Internal Revenue Service, 52
International Money Laundering
Abatement and Financial Anti-
Terrorism Act of 2001, 51-52
Iraq, 1991 military action against, 19
Islamic terrorism, 19-20, 22-23
See also September 11 attacks

Japanese-American internment, 18-19
Justice Department, 28-29, 50-51, 53-54

Karzai, Hamid, 37
Kenya, embassy bombing in, 20, 22-23

Leahy, Patrick J., 45, 51
Lindh, John Walker, 37

Military
and Afghanistan war, 35-36, 37, 39
and domestic security, 13, 41, 47
and Secretary of Defense, 30-31
Military tribunals, 51
Moussaoui, Zacarias, 28, 51
Mubarak, Hosni, 33-34
Musharraf, Pervez, 34

National Guard, 13, 41, 47
North American Aerospace Defense
Command (NORAD), 10-11, 41
North Atlantic Treaty Organization, 33
Northern Alliance, 34, 36

Office of National Preparedness, 27
Operation Enduring Freedom, 36
Operation Green Quest, 52

Pakistan, and Afghanistan war, 34
Pearl Harbor, Japanese raid on, 17-18
Pennsylvania, September 11 crash in, 10
Pentagon, September 11 attack on, 10, 11
Powell, Colin, 30, 54

Rahman, Omar Abdel, 20
Rice, Condoleezza, 11, 13, 29-31, 36
Ridge, Tom, 31, 42-43
Roosevelt, Franklin D., 18

Ross, Christopher, 36
Rove, Karl, 11
Rumsfeld, Donald, 30-31, 35, 36
Russia, and Afghanistan war, 34-35

September 11 attacks, 9-10
and Ashcroft, 28
blame and retribution for, 13-14,
47, 49-50, 51
casualties in, 10, 14
and CIA, 13, 26
first day's response to, 10-13
and fundraising efforts, 14
and rescue workers, 12, 14
security after, 10-13, 41, 47
terrorists involved in, 28, 51
See also Afghanistan war; Domestic
security; Terrorism, war on
Shadow Government, 11, 13, 47
Spann, Mike, 37

Taliban, 34, 36, 37, 39, 54
Tanzania, embassy bombing in, 20, 22-23
Tenet, George, 26
Terrorism, war on, 14, 49-55
and Bush, 49
and cabinet, 27, 28-31
and courts, 50-51, 53-54
and detainees, 28-29, 50-51, 53-54
and financial support of terrorists,
51-53
and intelligence, 26, 50, 51
and military tribunals, 51
and surveillance, 50
See also Afghanistan war; Domestic
security
Transportation Security Administration,
43-44
Treasury Department, 51-52

United Nations, 12, 33
U.S.A. Patriot Act, 50-51, 53

World Trade Center, terrorist attacks
on, 9-10, 19-20
World War II, 18

Yousef, Ramzi, 20

page:
2: AP/Wide World Photos	32: AP/Wide World Photos
8: AP/Wide World Photos	35: AP/Wide World Photos
12: AP/Wide World Photos	38: AP/Wide World Photos
15: AP/Wide World Photos	40: AP/Wide World Photos
16: AP/Wide World Photos	43: AP/Wide World Photos
21: AP/Wide World Photos	46: AP/Wide World Photos
22: AP/Wide World Photos	48: AP/Wide World Photos
24: AP/Wide World Photos	52: AP/Wide World Photos
29: AP/Wide World Photos	55: AP/Wide World Photos
30: AP/Wide World Photos	

Cover: AFP/Corbis

ANGELA VALDEZ lives in Philadelphia, Pennsylvania. A graduate of New York University, she has reported for several newspapers, including *Newsday*, *The Flint Journal* and *The Philadelphia Inquirer*. She is now working toward her Ph.D. in U.S. history at the University of Pennsylvania.